Sheffield Ontario and Area in Photos, Saving Our History One Photo at a Time

Photography
by Barbara Raué
2012

Series Name:
Cruising Ontario

Book 14: Sheffield and Area

Cover photo: Sheffield Home

Series Name: Cruising Ontario

Book 1: London
Book 2: Dundas
Book 3: Hamilton
Book 4: Oakville
Book 5: Chesley
Book 6: Stoney Creek
Book 7: Waterdown
Book 8: Owen Sound
Book 9: Mount Forest
Book 10: Dundalk
Book 11: Burford and Area
Book 12: Waterford and Area
Book 13: Drumbo and Area
Book 14: Sheffield and Area
Book 15: Tavistock and Area

Other Books by Barbara Raue

Coins and Gems

Arrows, Indians and Love

The Life and Times of Barbara
Volume 1: Inventions That Have Enhanced My Life
Volume 2: Entertainment That I Have Enjoyed
Volume 3: East Coast Trip 2009
Volume 4: Olympics
Volume 5: Wonders of the World

Sheffield

Sheffield, located 35 kilometres from the city core, is part of the municipality of Hamilton. Sheffield was settled by the early 1800s and the village was found by Reverend John A. Cornell who immigrated from Dutchess County, New York in 1809. In 1834 he built the first local church on the site where the United Church is now located.

Kirkwall

Kirkwall is located about 13 kilometres east of Cambridge.

Westfield Heritage Village

Westfield Heritage Village is located at 1049 Kirkwall Road off Highway 8 west of Rockton. It has over thirty historical buildings which have been restored.

Sheffield Homes and Barns

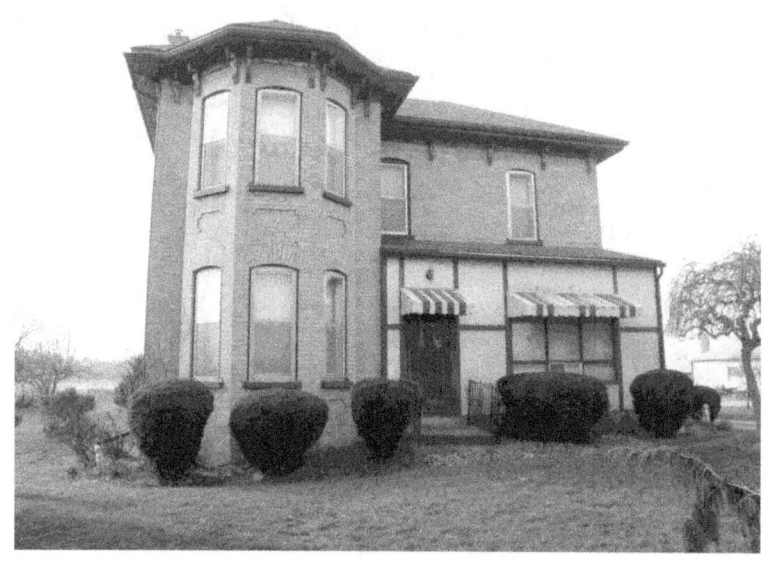

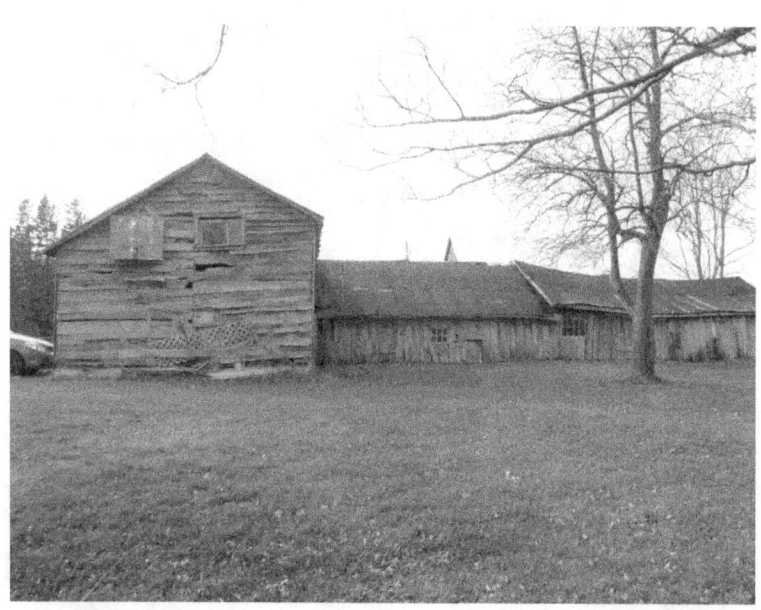

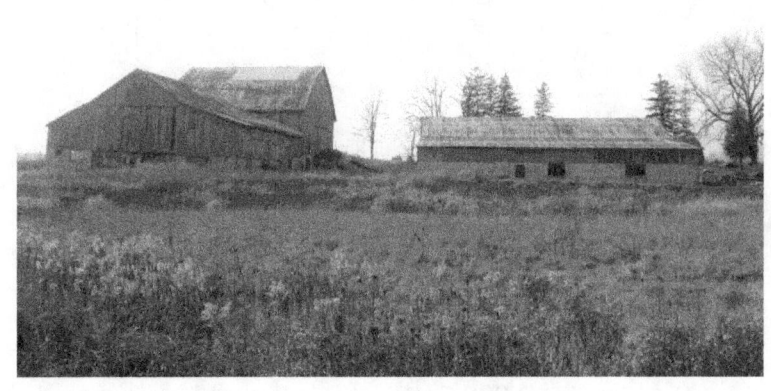

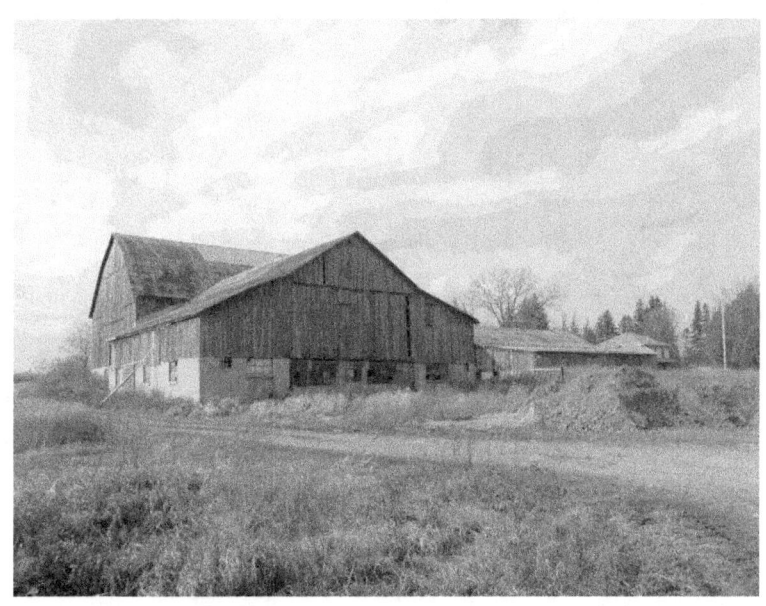

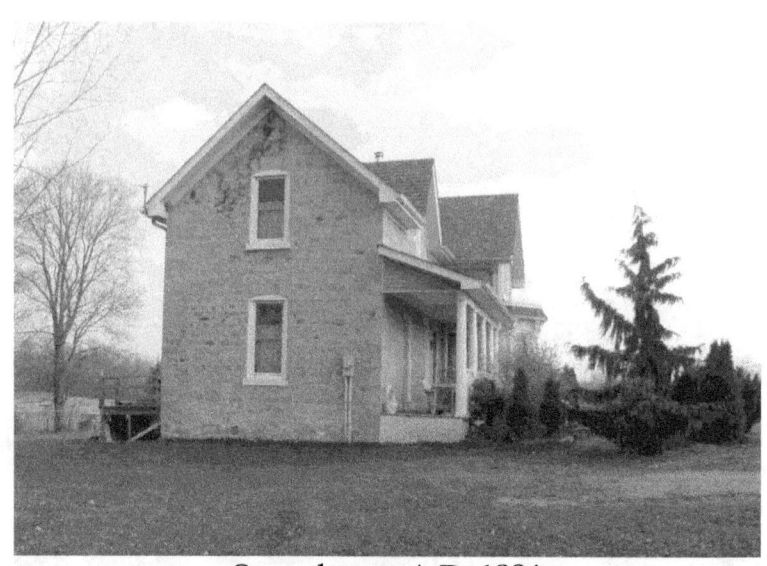

Stone house A.D. 1884
908 Settlers Road

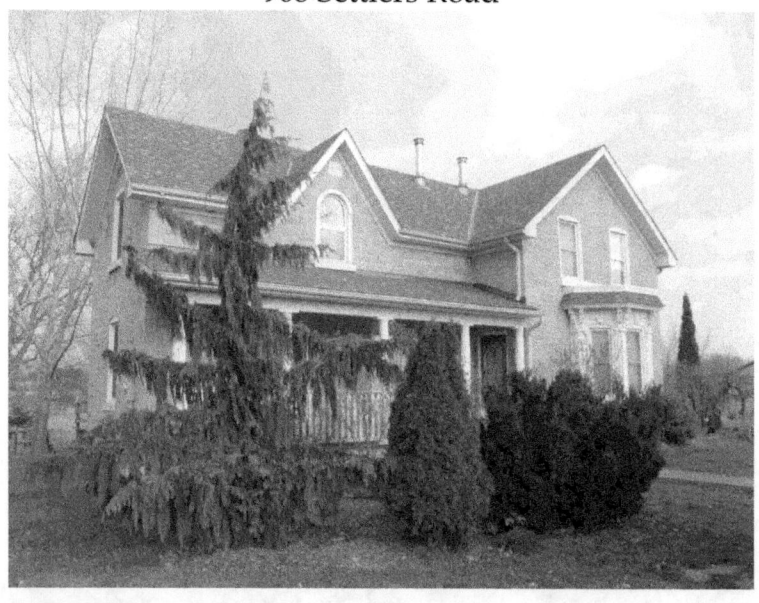

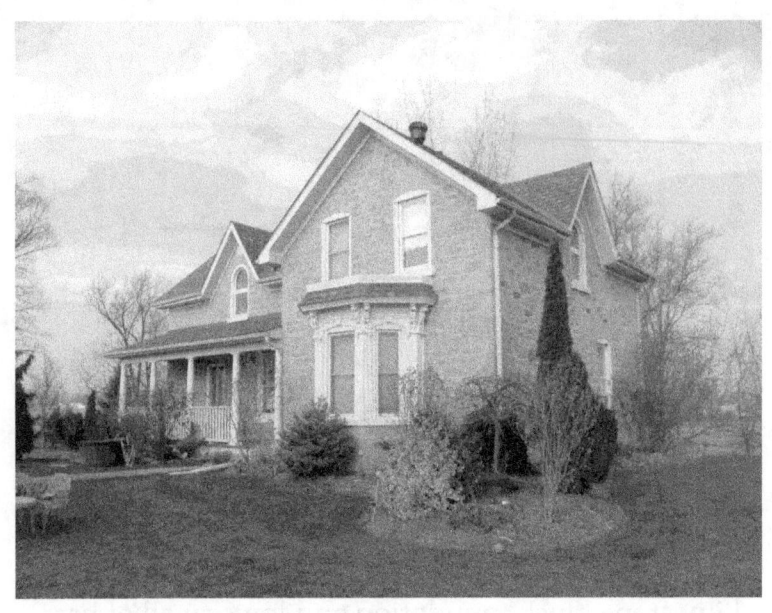

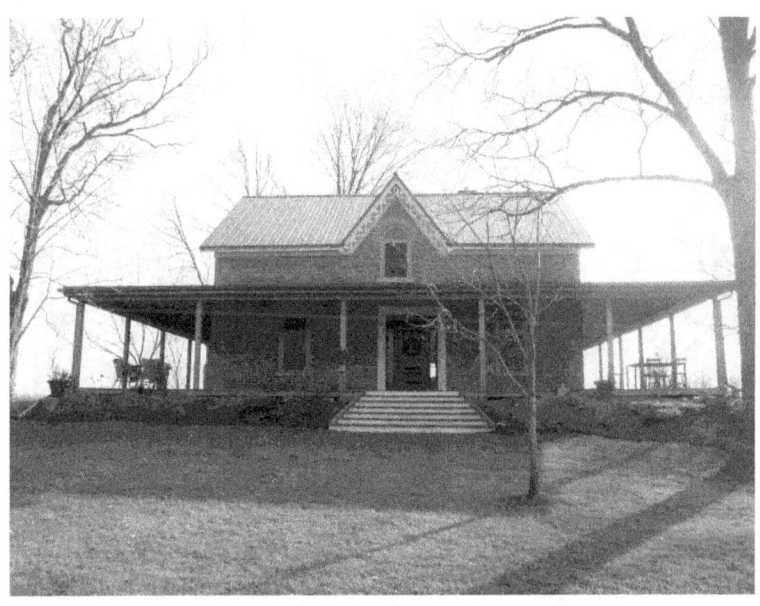

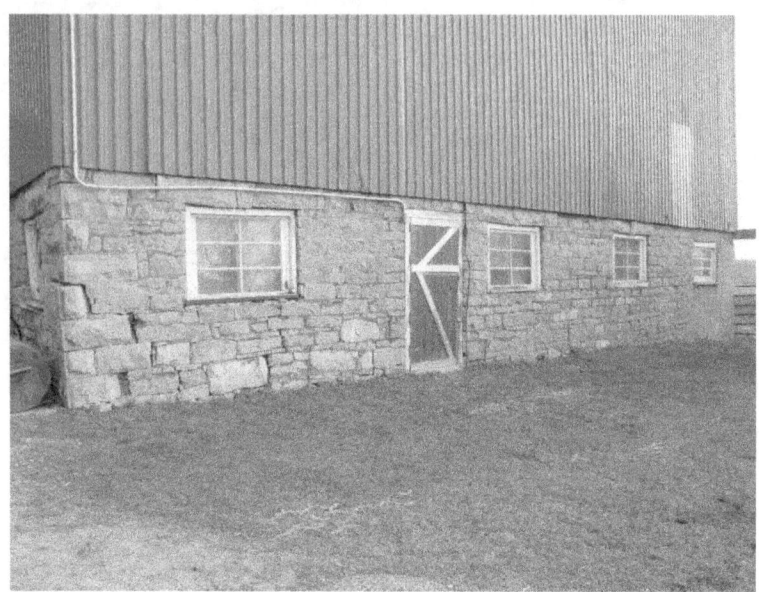

Limestone block foundation and lower wall of barn

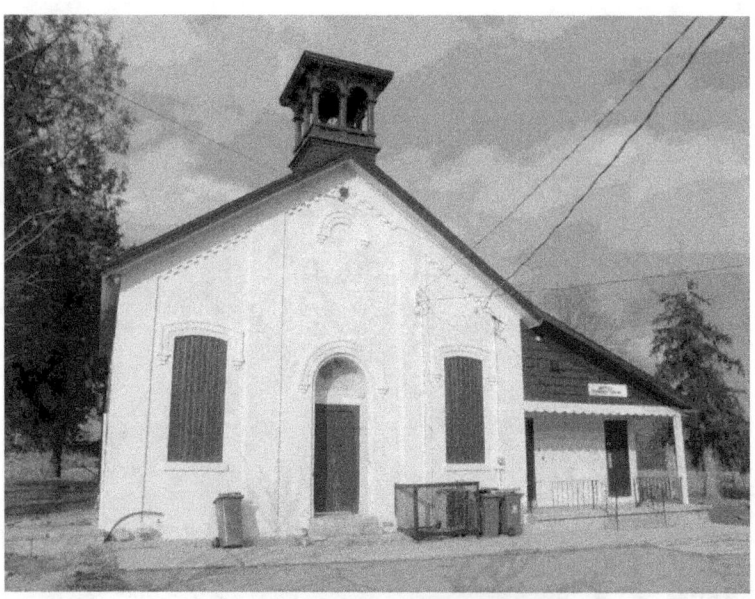

School Section No. 9 – 1877

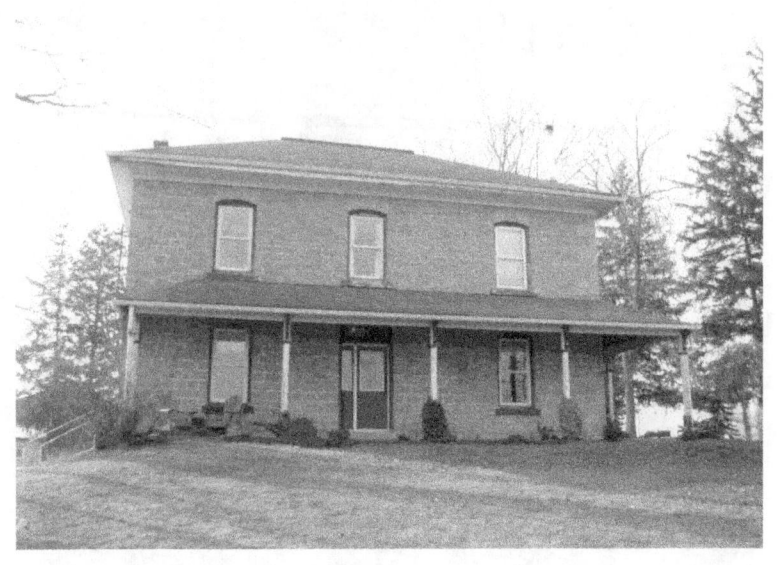

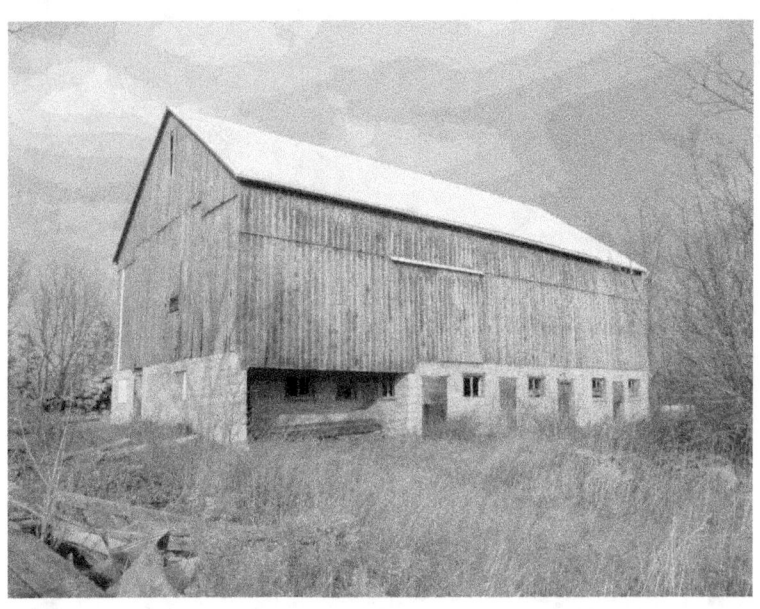

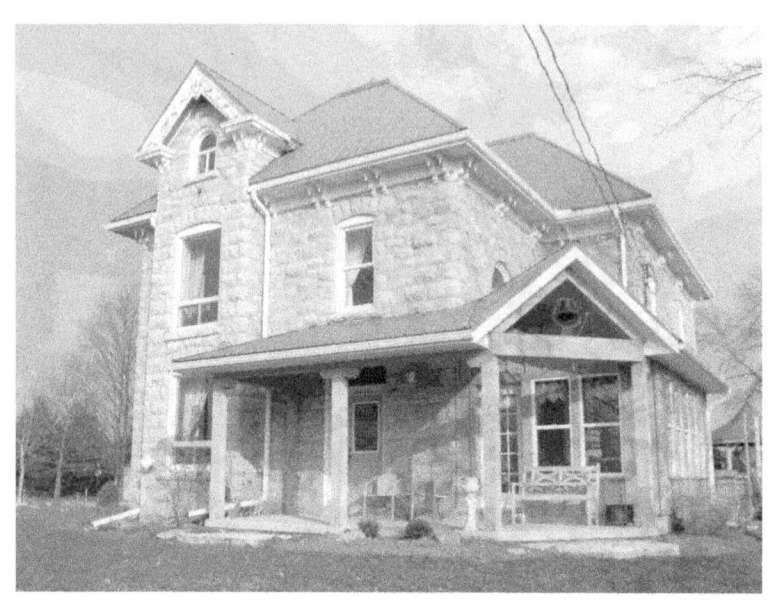

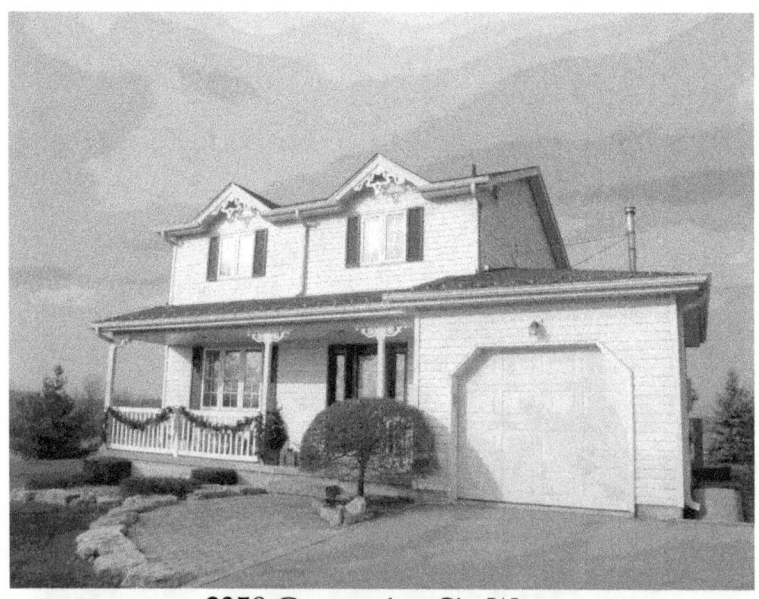

2359 Concession Six West

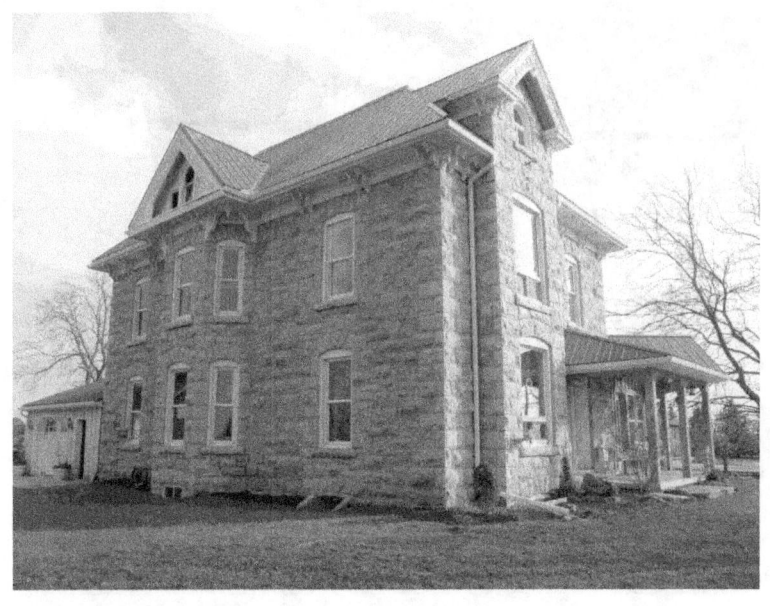

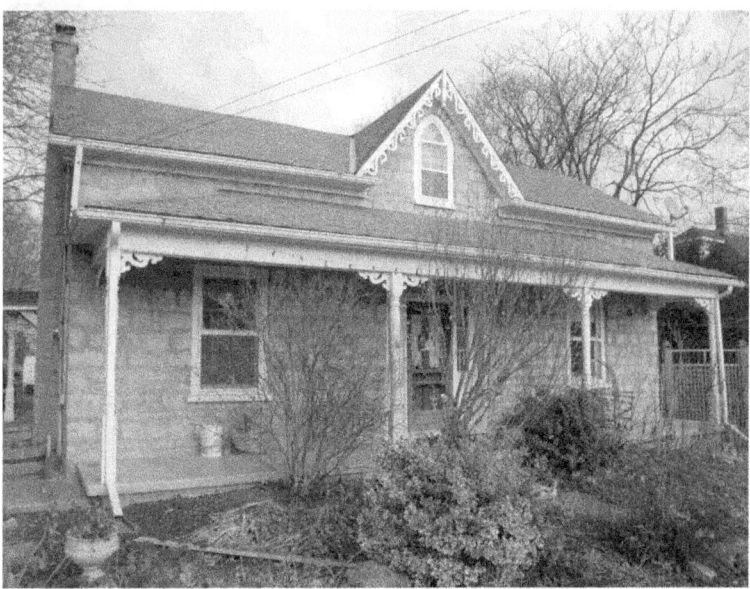

Gothic Style centre arch with gingerbread trim

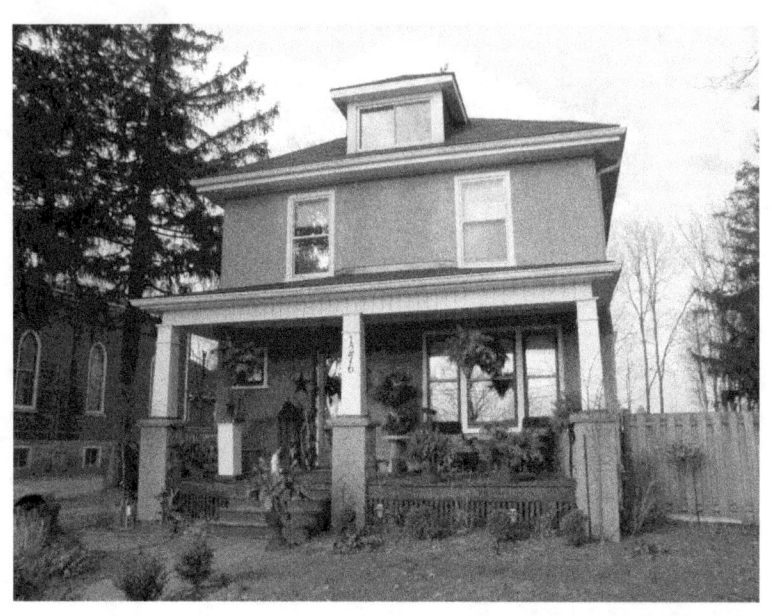

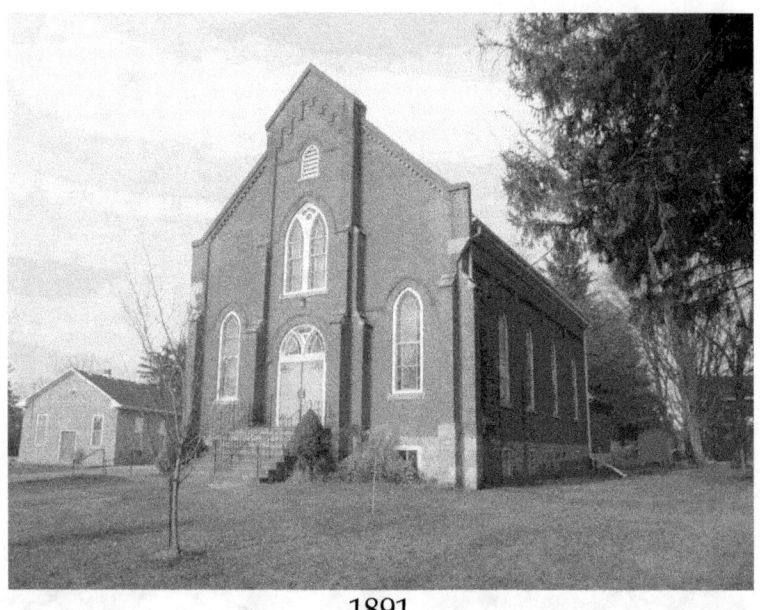

1891

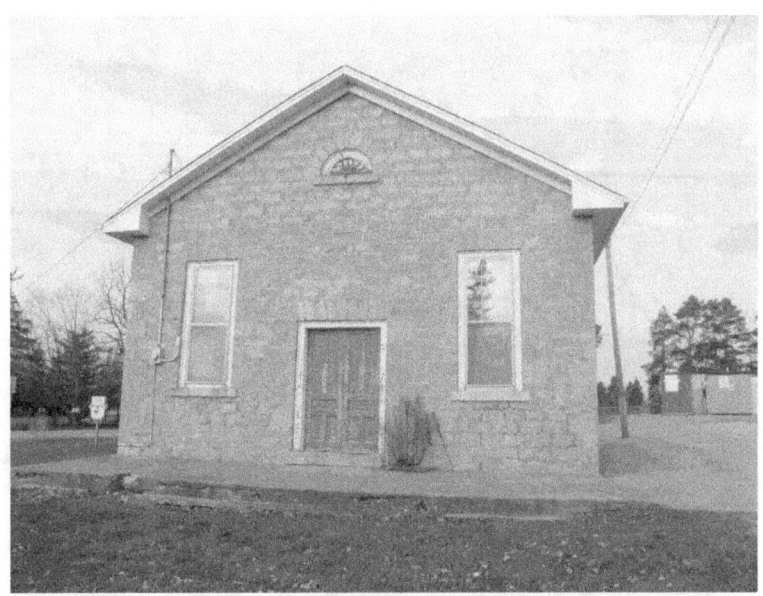

A.D. 1862

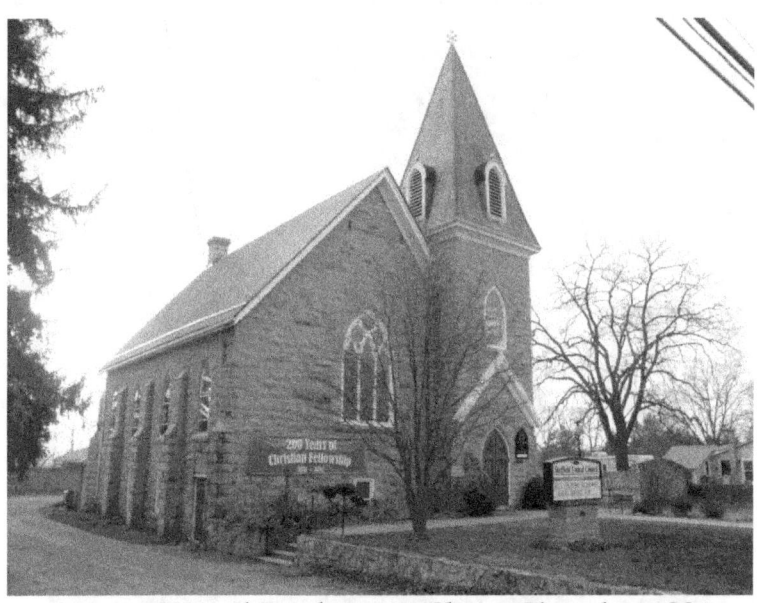

Former United Brethren in Christ Church – 1894
Sheffield United Church
200 Years of Christian Fellowship 1812-2012

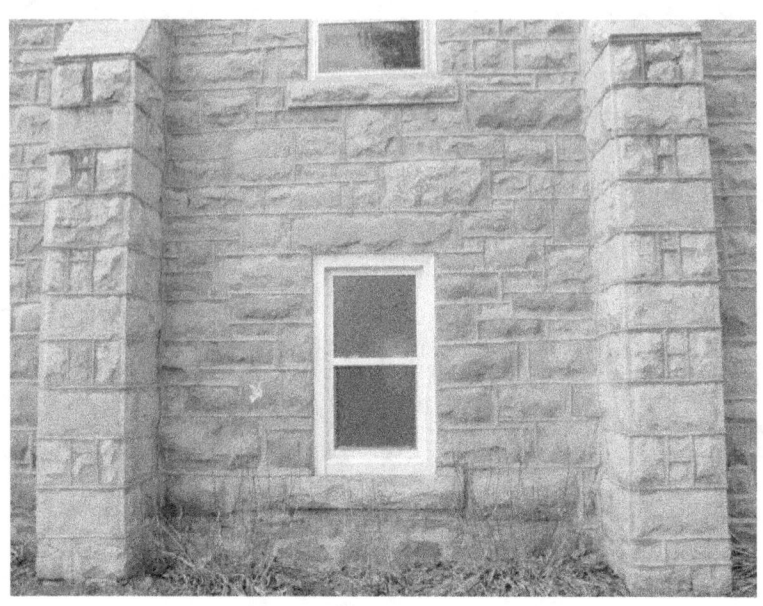

Sheffield United Church

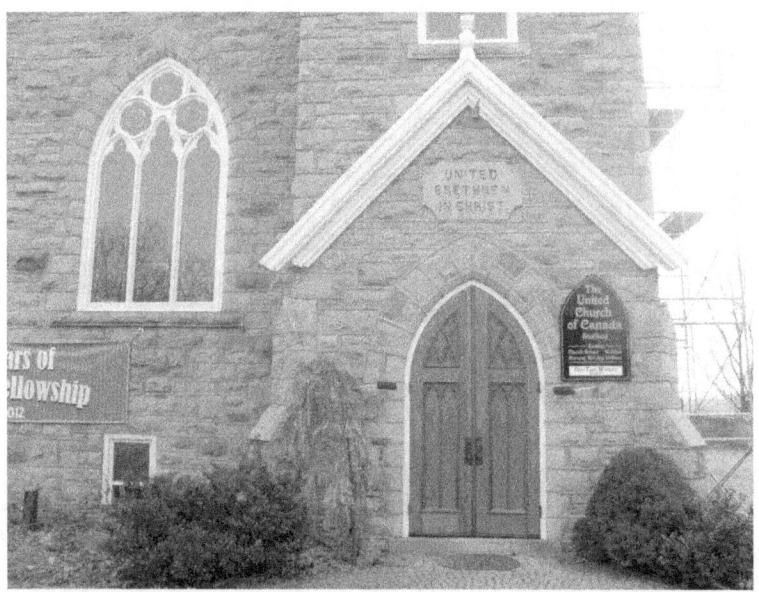

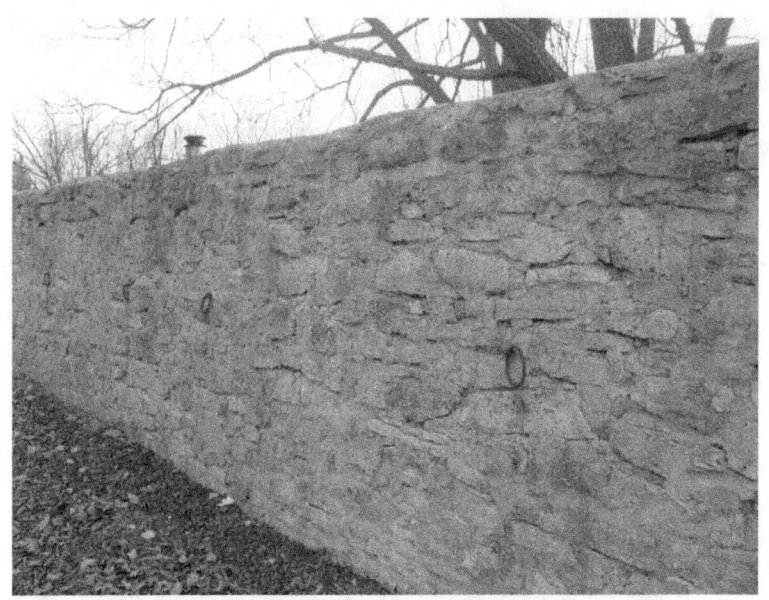

Rings in the wall for tying up the horses
Sheffield United Church

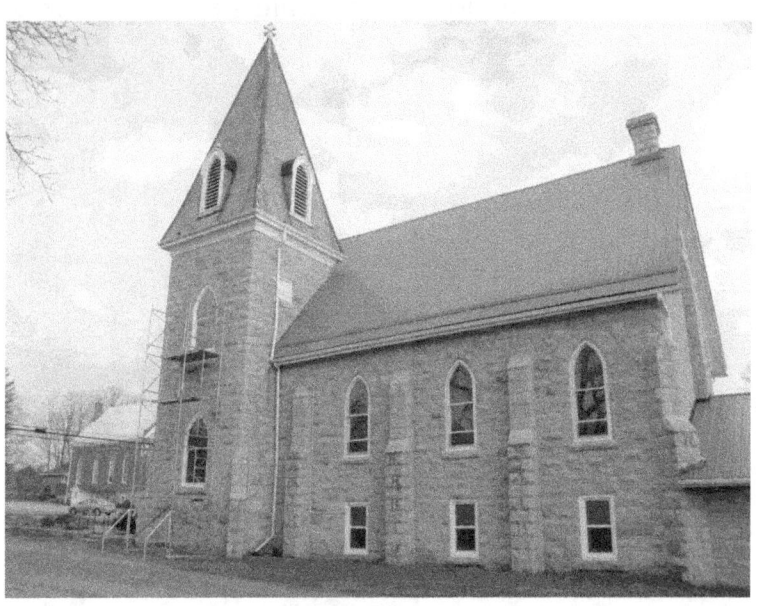

Kirkwall

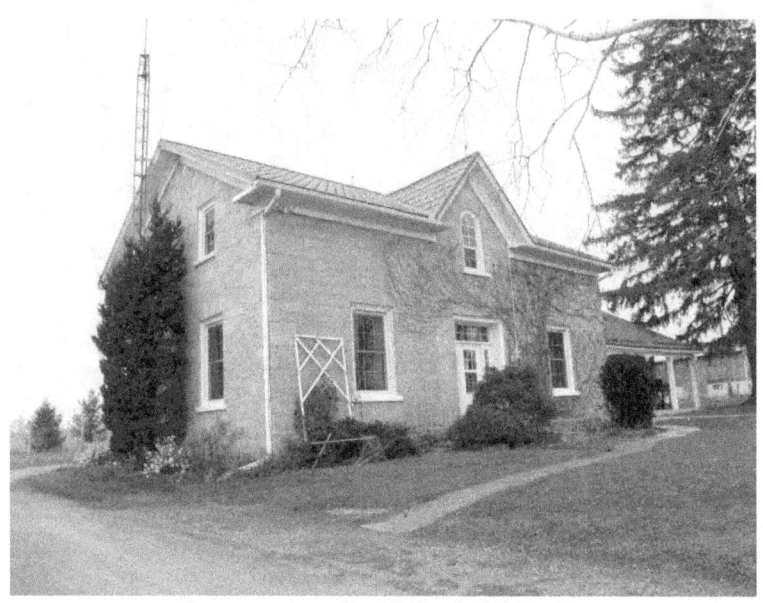

Concession 8 – Fairchild Farm

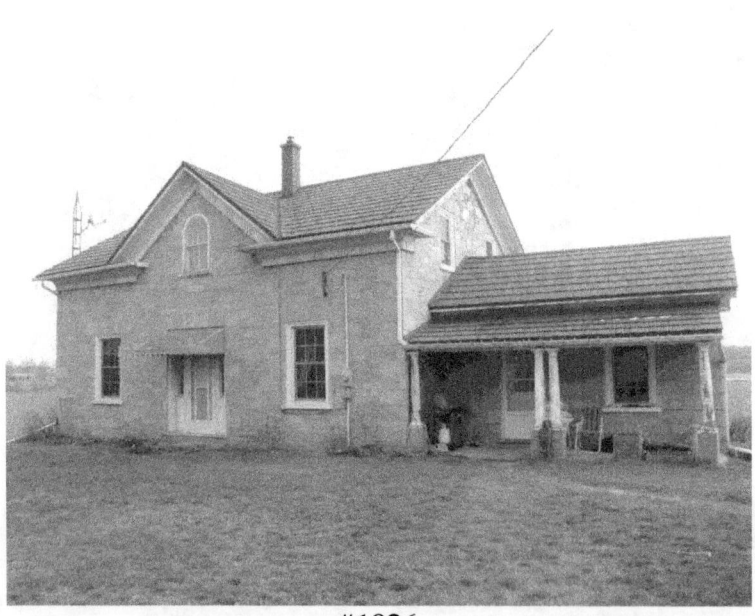

#1926

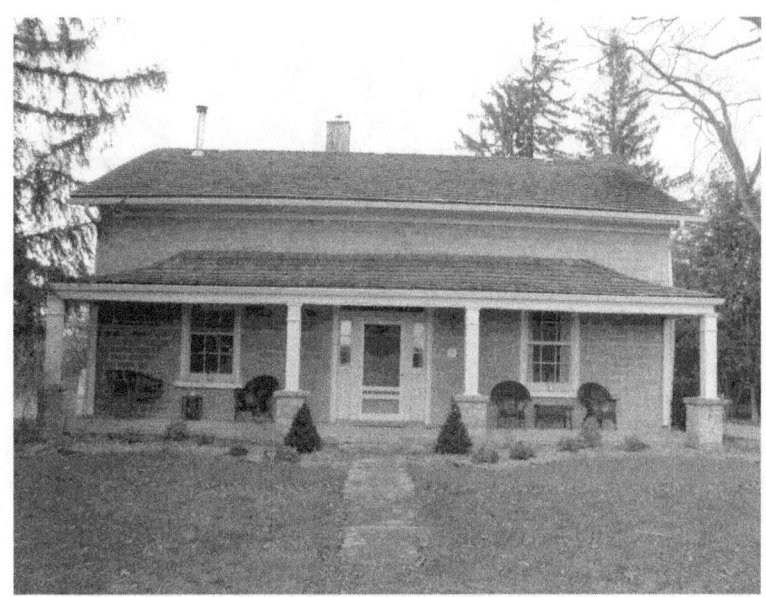

#1905

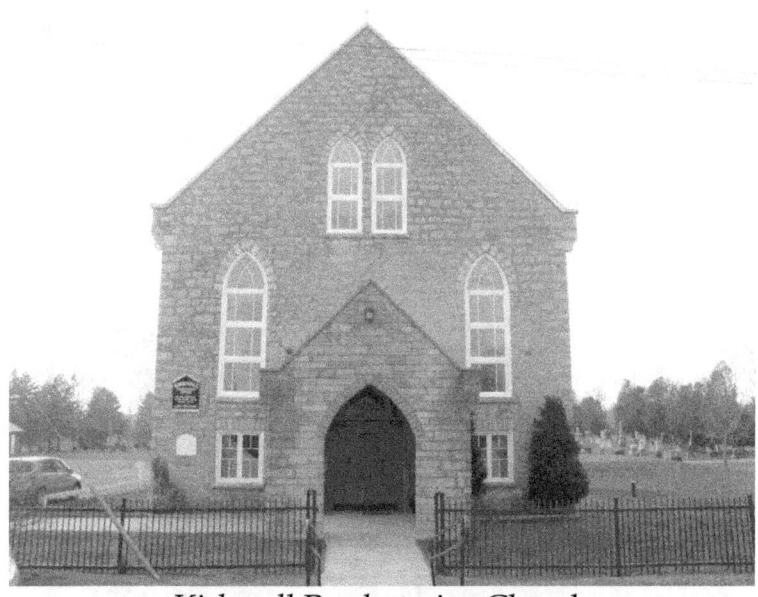

Kirkwall Presbyterian Church
1886 Concession 8 West and Kirkwall Road
Built 1848, Remodelled 1900

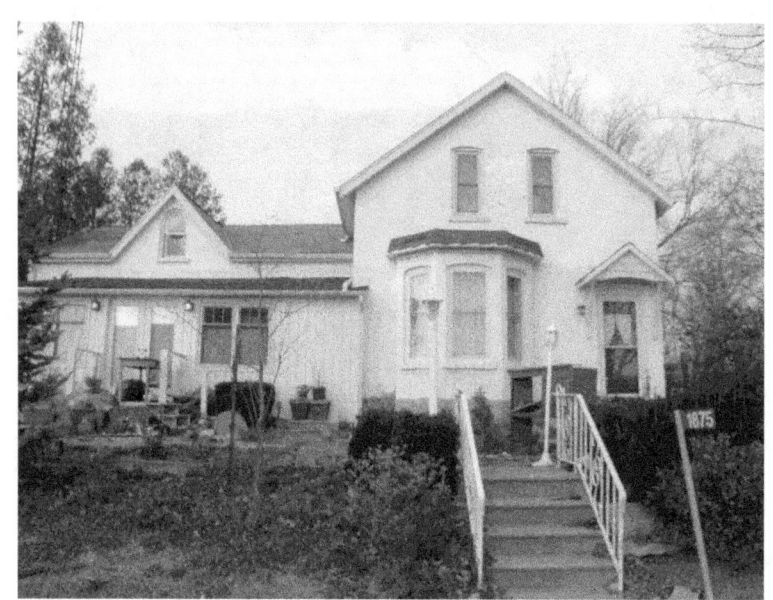

#1875

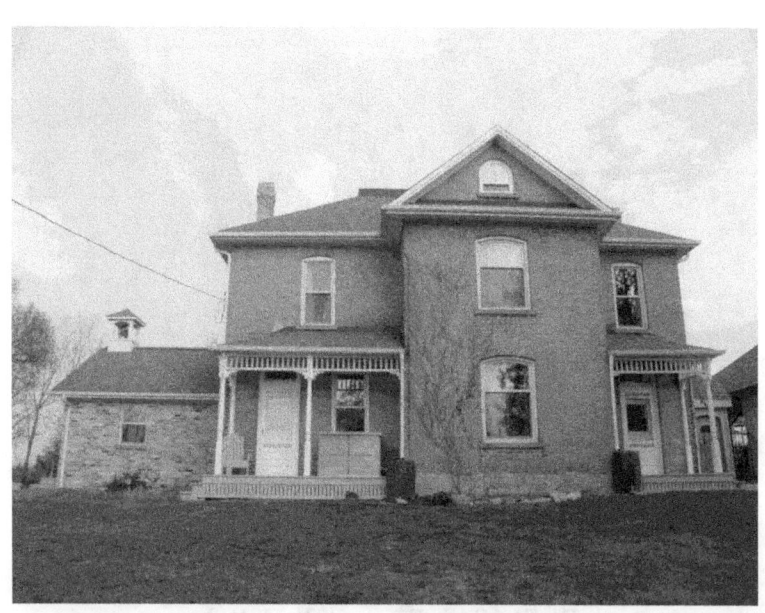

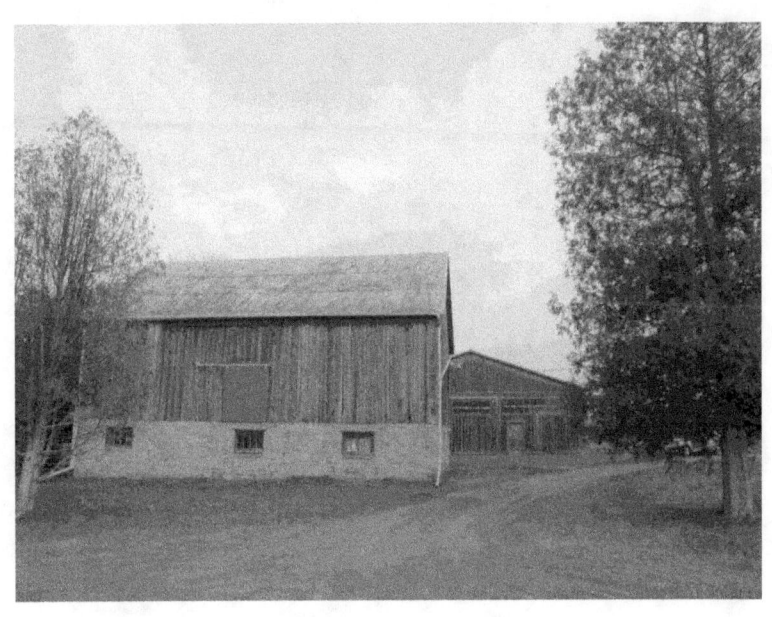

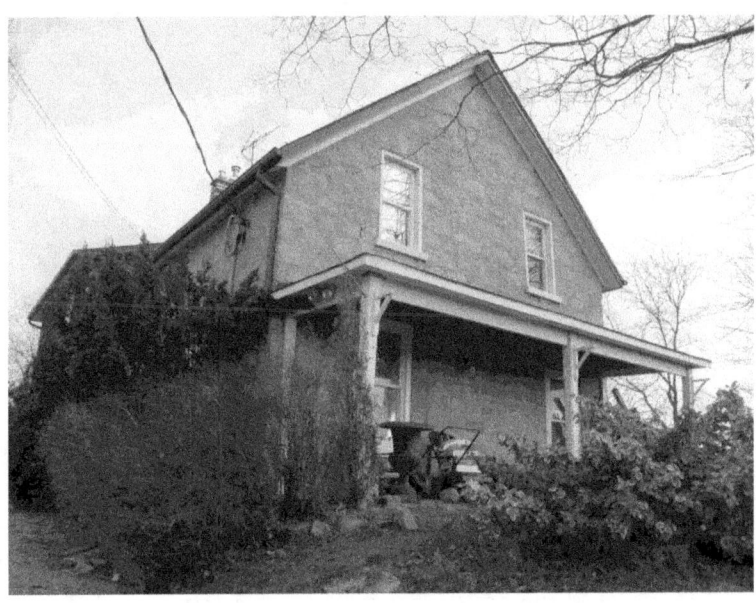

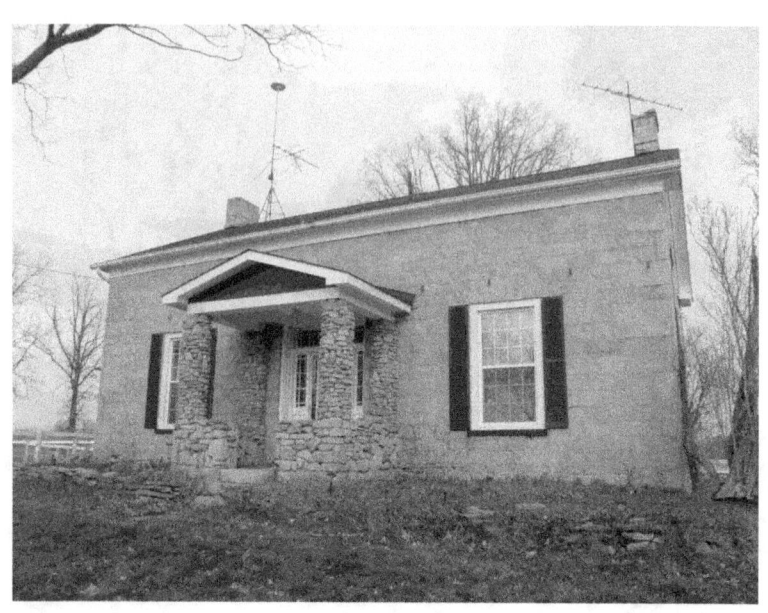

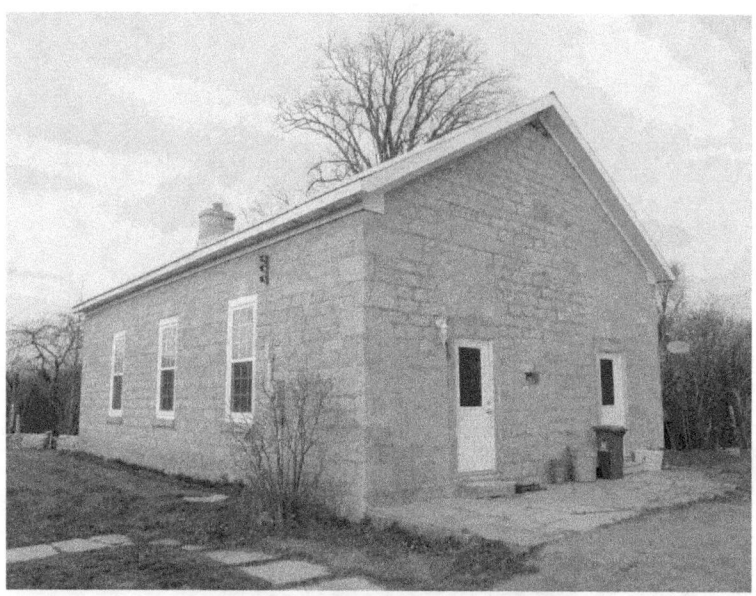

1434 Kirkwall Road – c. 1862

Westfield Heritage Village

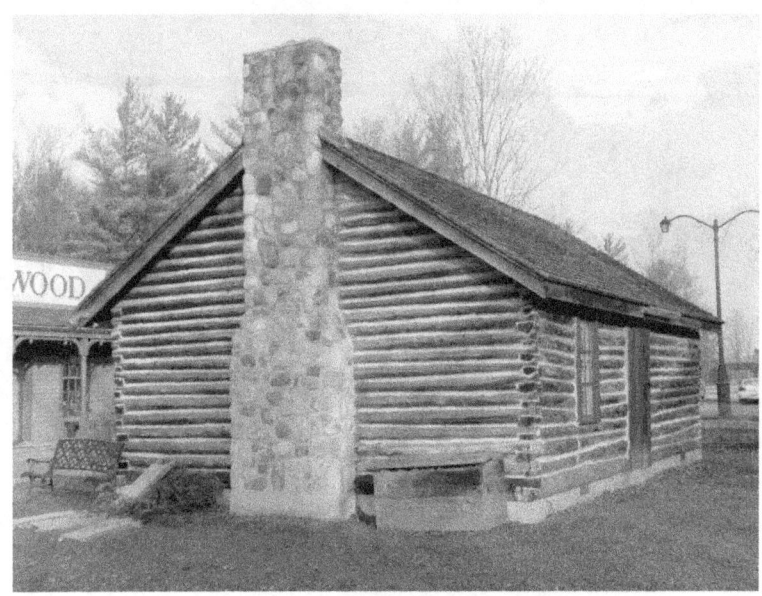

Log cabin

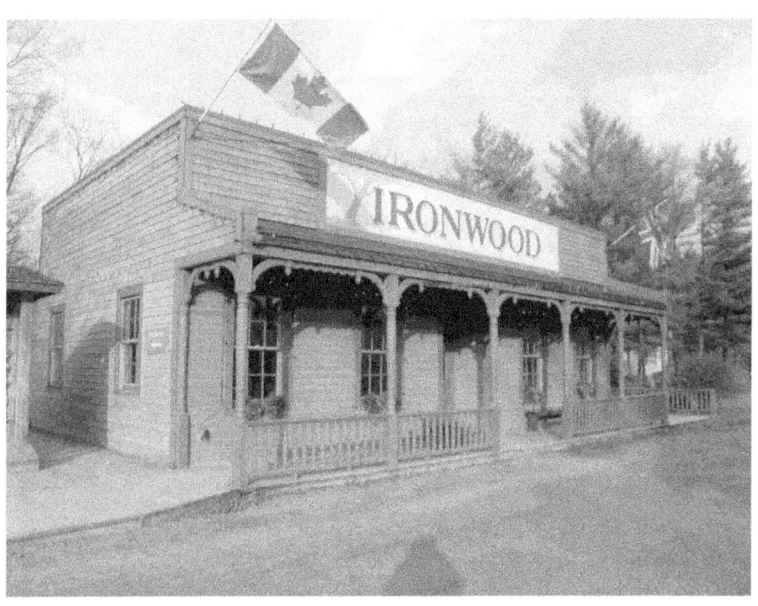

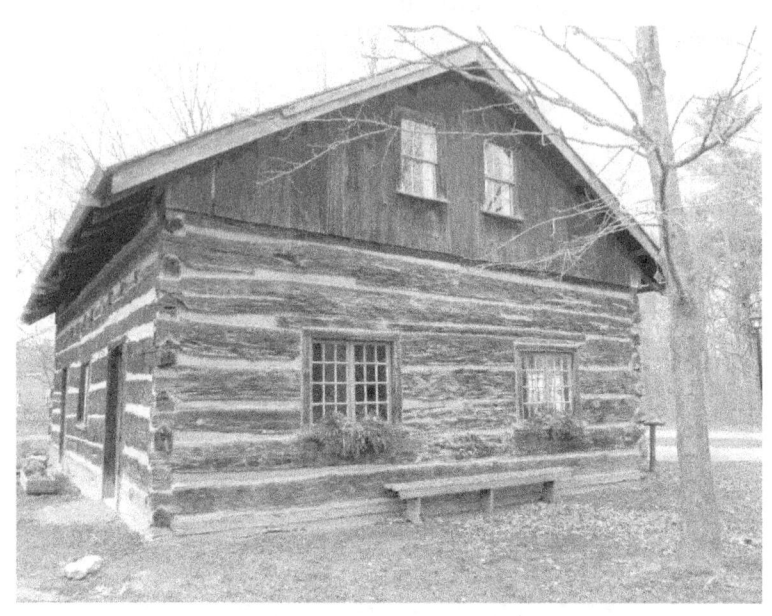

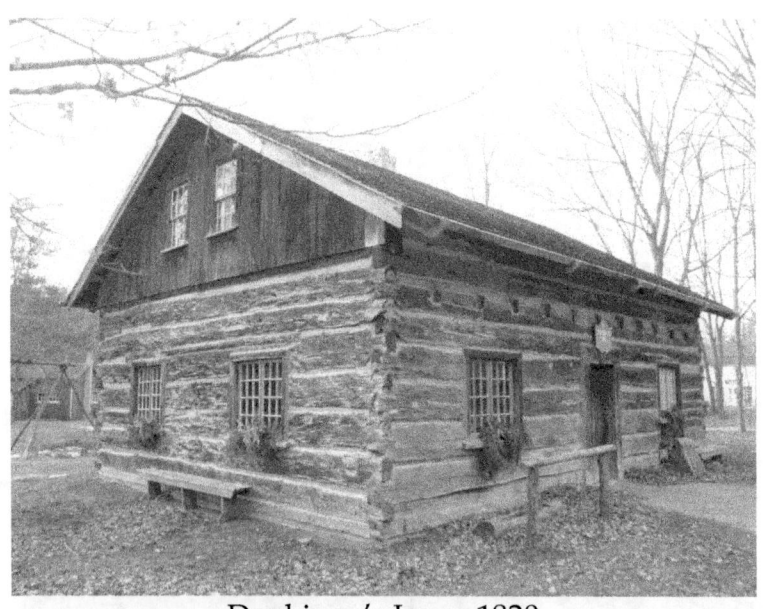

Daubigny's Inn c. 1820

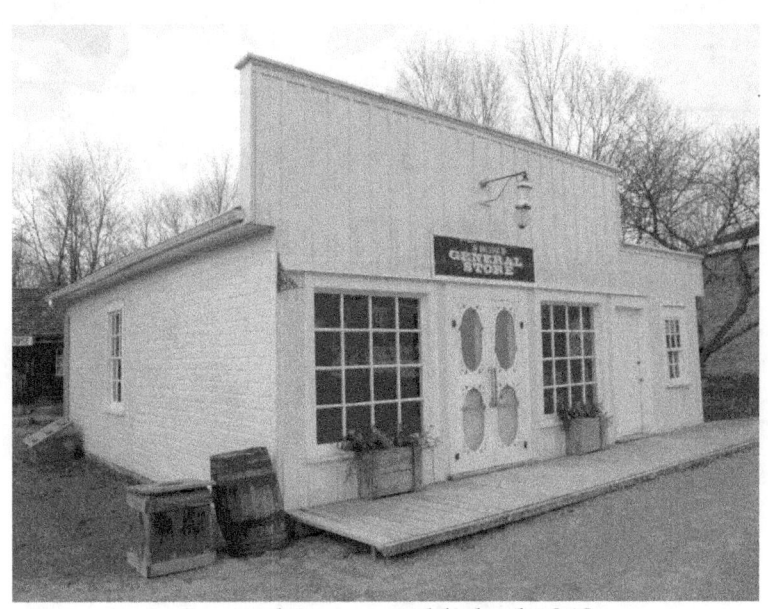

General Store established 1848

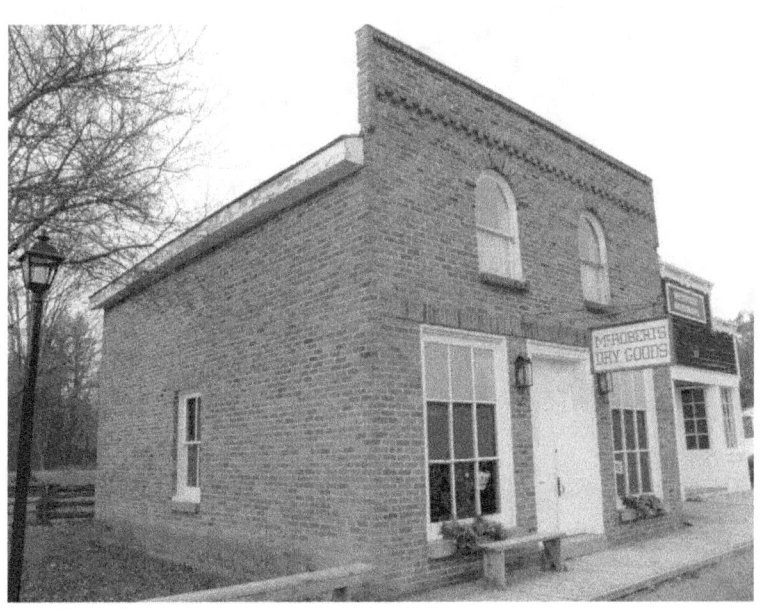

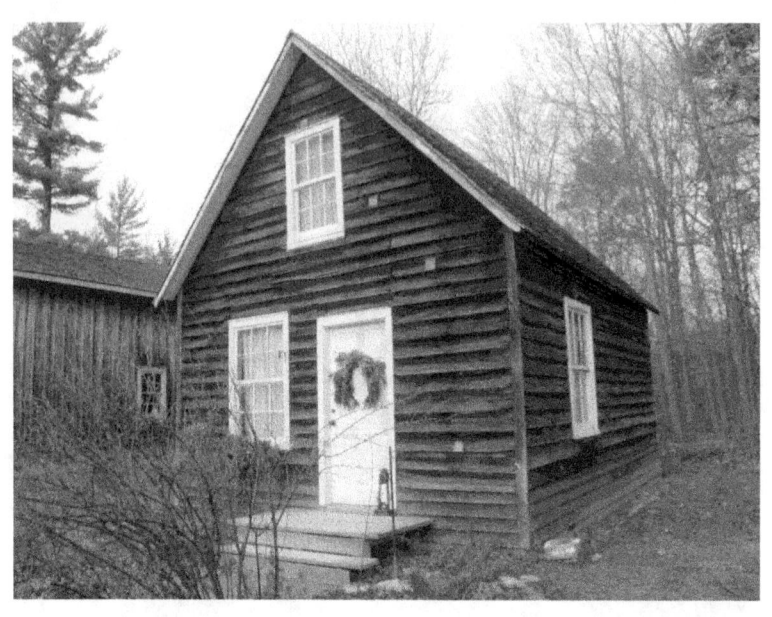

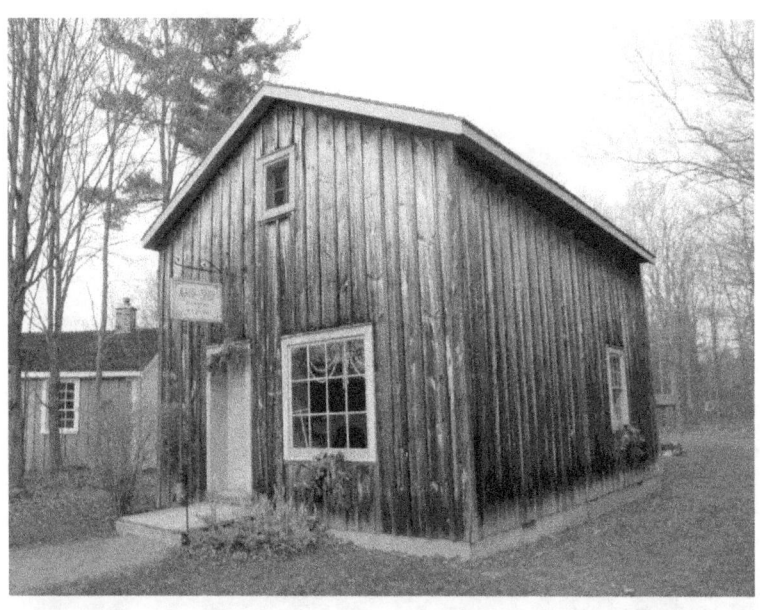

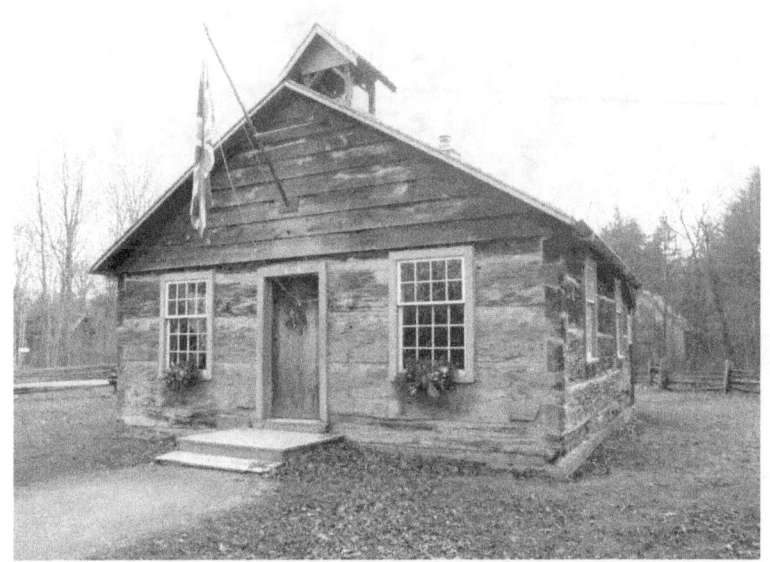

S.S. 24 Burford Township School c. 1845 – Brant County

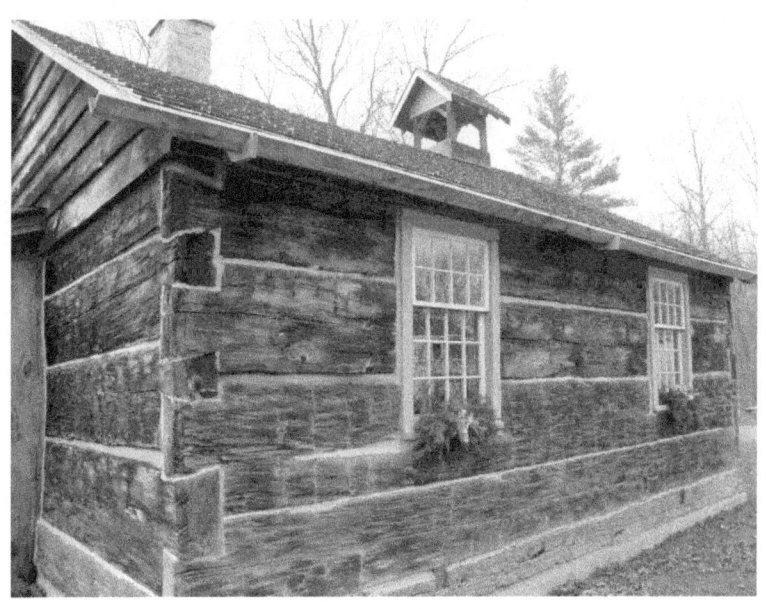

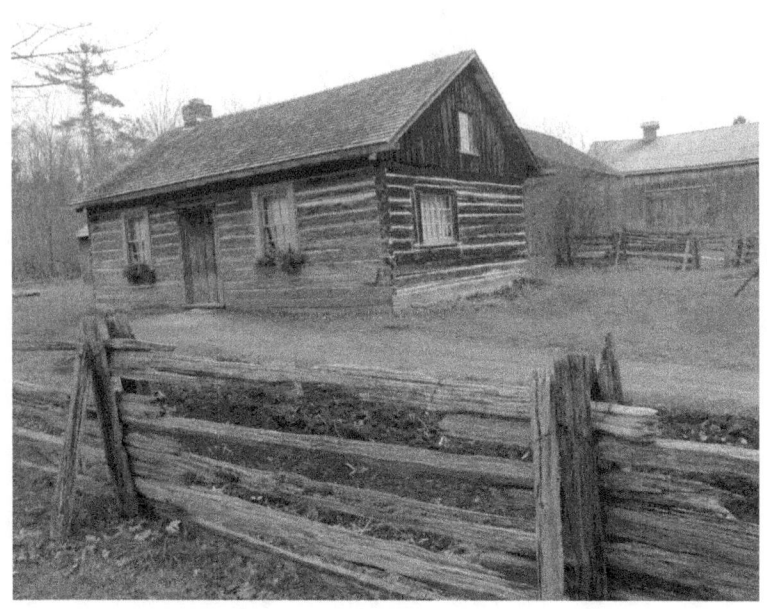

Lockhart House – 1845 – Oxford County

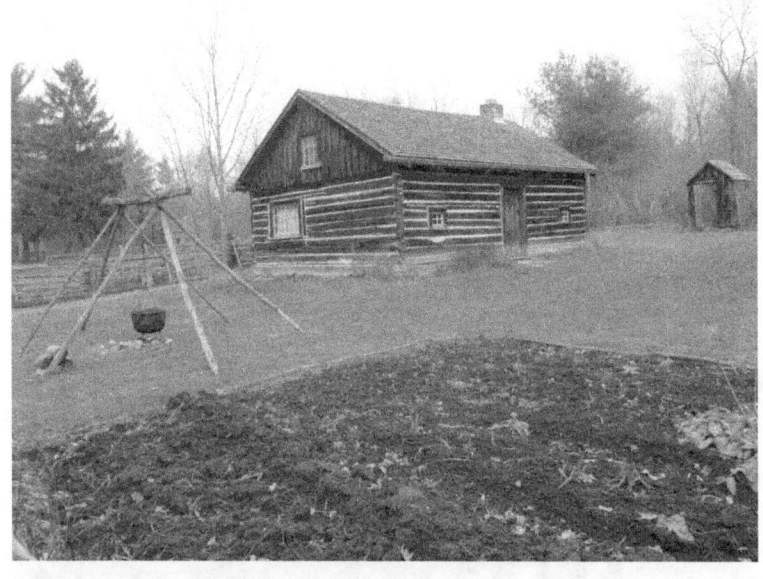

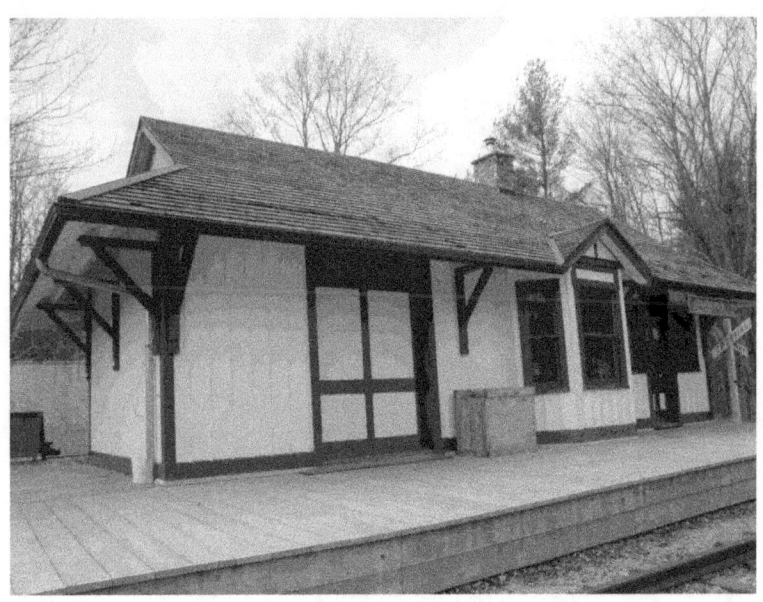

The Jerseyville Railway Station was built in 1896 when ten trains a day ran between Hamilton and Brantford.

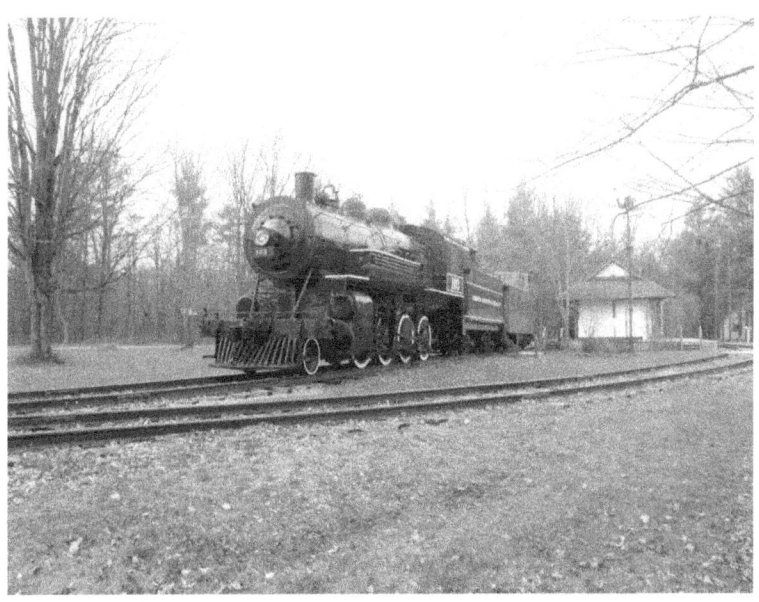

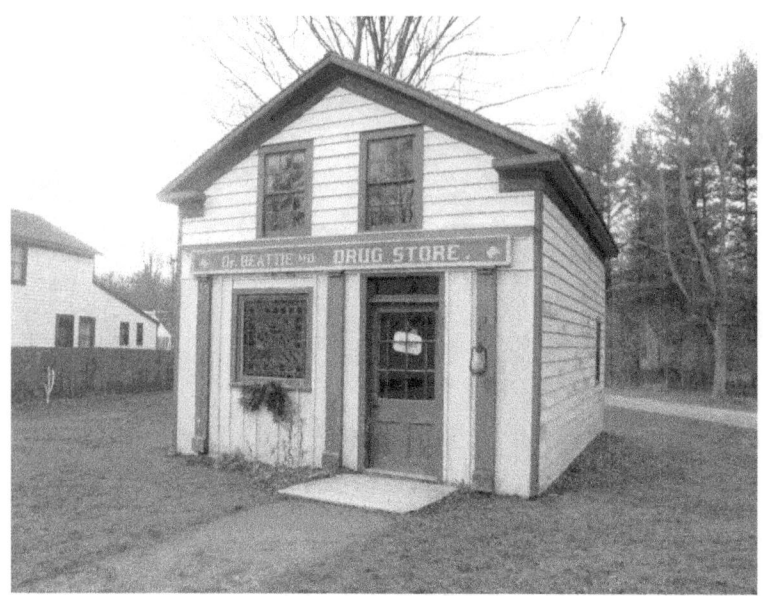

Clapboard building

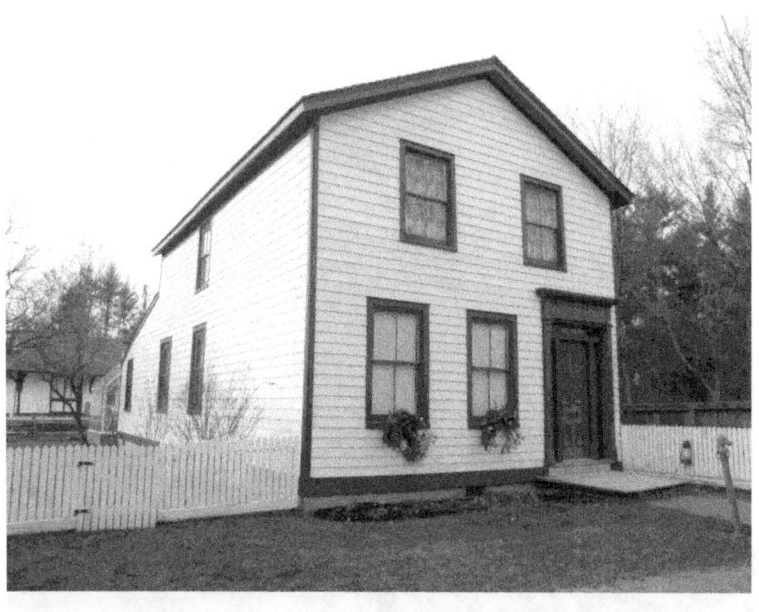

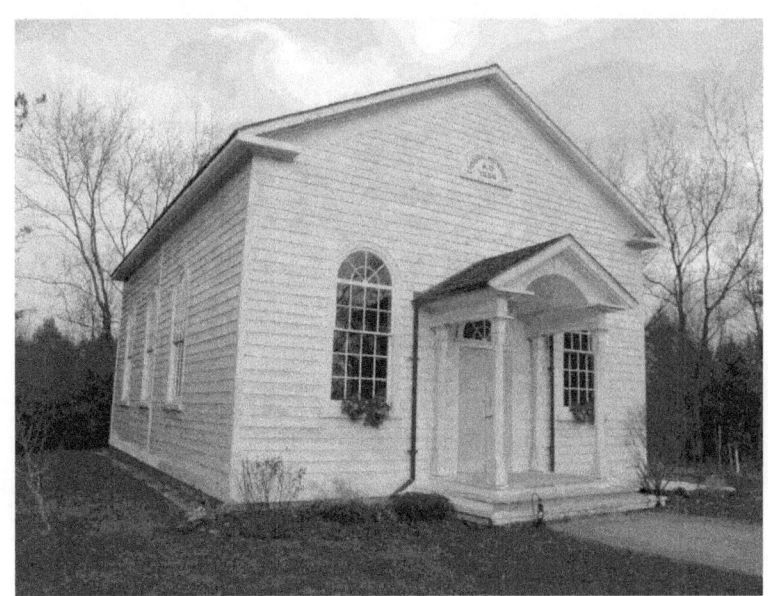

Episcopal Methodist Church A.D. 1854

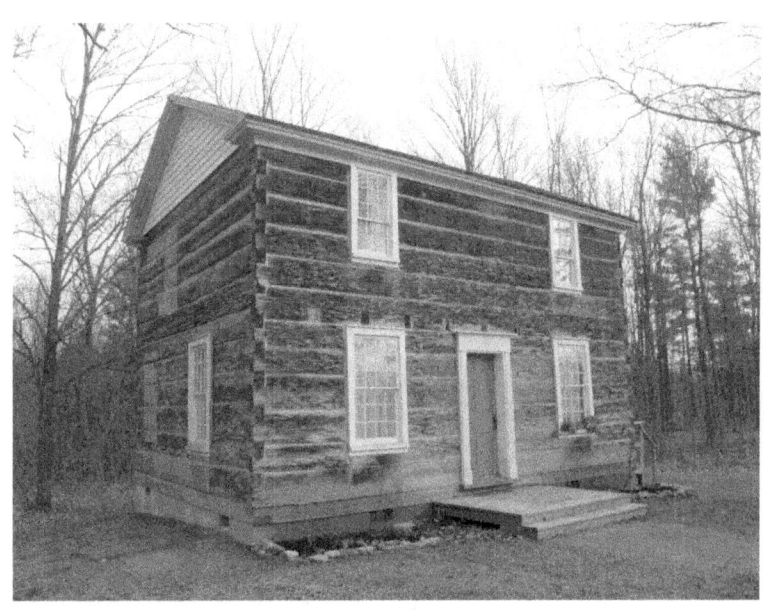

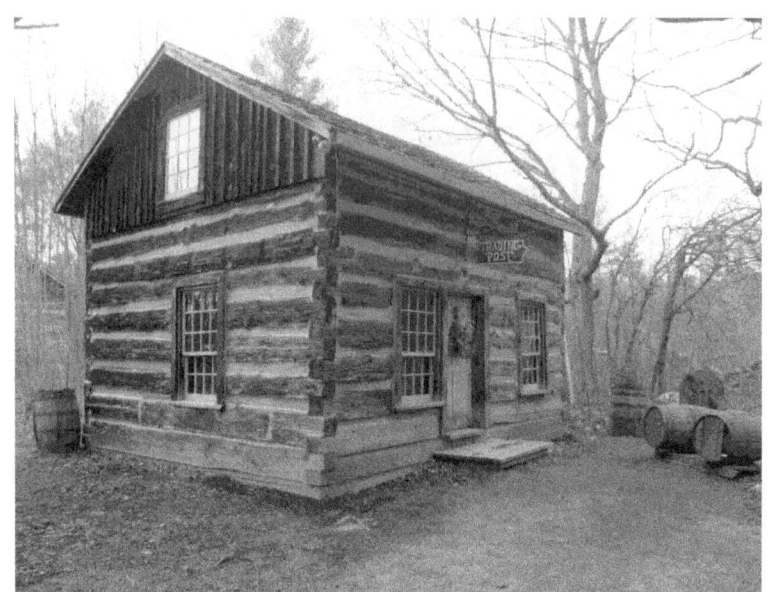

Trading Post

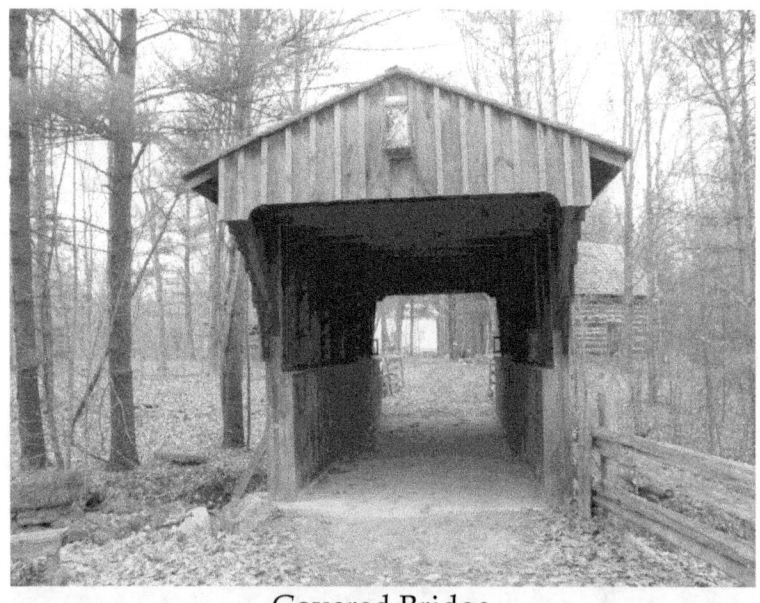

Covered Bridge

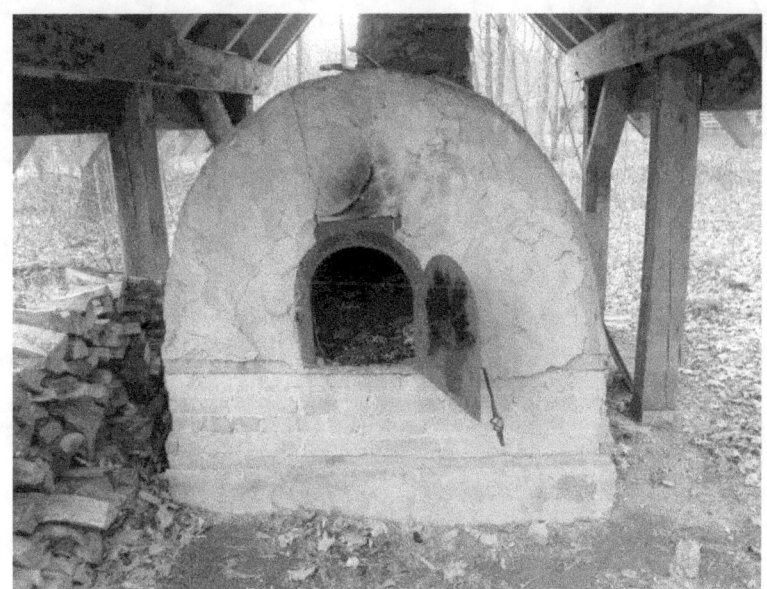

Outdoor oven

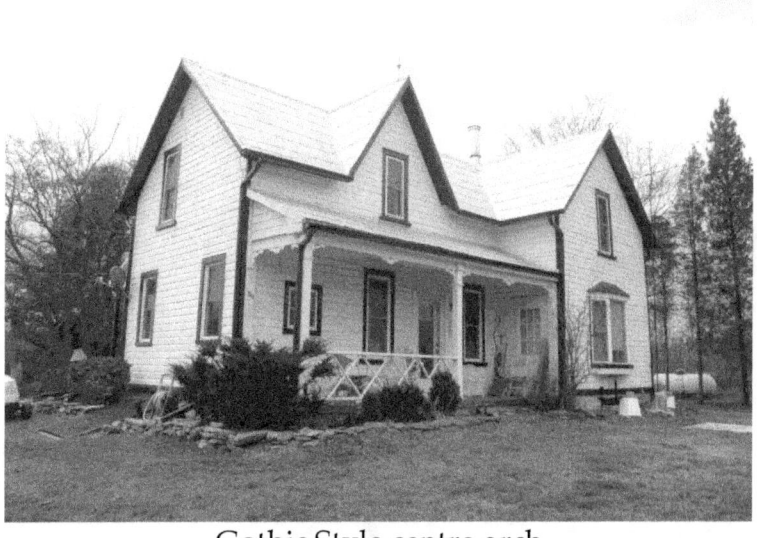

Gothic Style centre arch